FUN EXPERIMENTS WITH SCIENCE AND MATHS

on the Move

Roy Richards

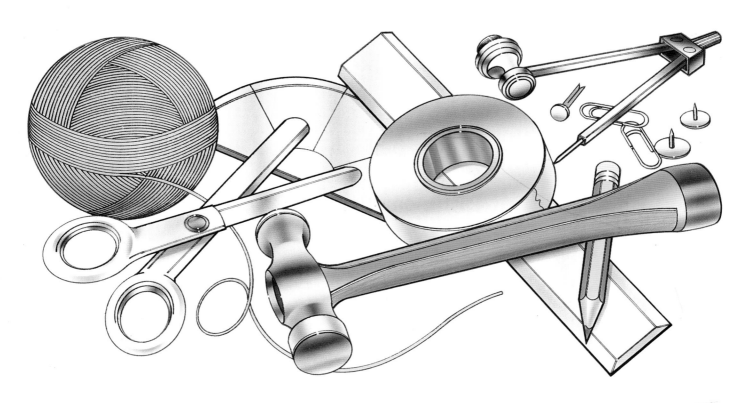

SIMON & SCHUSTER

LONDON • SYDNEY • NEW YORK • TOKYO • SINGAPORE • TORONTO

Contents

First published in 1990
by Simon & Schuster Young Books

Simon & Schuster Young Books
Simon & Schuster Ltd
Wolsey House, Wolsey Road
Hemel Hempstead, Herts HP2 4SS

Text © 1990 Roy Richards
Illustrations © 1990 Simon & Schuster

Designed by David West
Children's Book Design
Illustrated by Alex Pang

Printed and bound in Belgium
by Proost International Book Production

British Library Cataloguing in Publication
Data
Richards, Roy
  On the move.
  1. Science. Experiments
  I. Title II. Series
  507.24

  ISBN 0-7500-0283-2

Paper plane	3
Paper dart	4–5
Delta wing	6
Acrobatic plane	7
Balsa wood glider	8
Jet rocket and propeller-driven plane	9
Parachutes	10
Paper spinners	11
Boomerangs	12
Windmills	13
Tin helicopter	14
Plastic helicopter	15
Kite	16
Hot-air balloon	17
Cotton-reel tank	18
Drink-can dragster	19
Land yacht	20
Trolley	21
Jumping Jack	22
Mouse on the move	23
Tops	24–25
Spinners	26–27
Paper boat	28
Balsa wood boats	29
Power-driven boats	30
Catamaran and trimaran	31
Notes for parents and teachers	32

PAPER PLANE

Take a sheet of A4 paper (210 x 297 millimetres).

1 Fold the two opposite corners together.

2 Fold the bottom edge up half the distance of "x".

3 Fold the paper in half along the dotted line.

4 Fold the bottom sections upward.

5 Fold the wings down along the dotted line.

6 Staple the nose and tail.

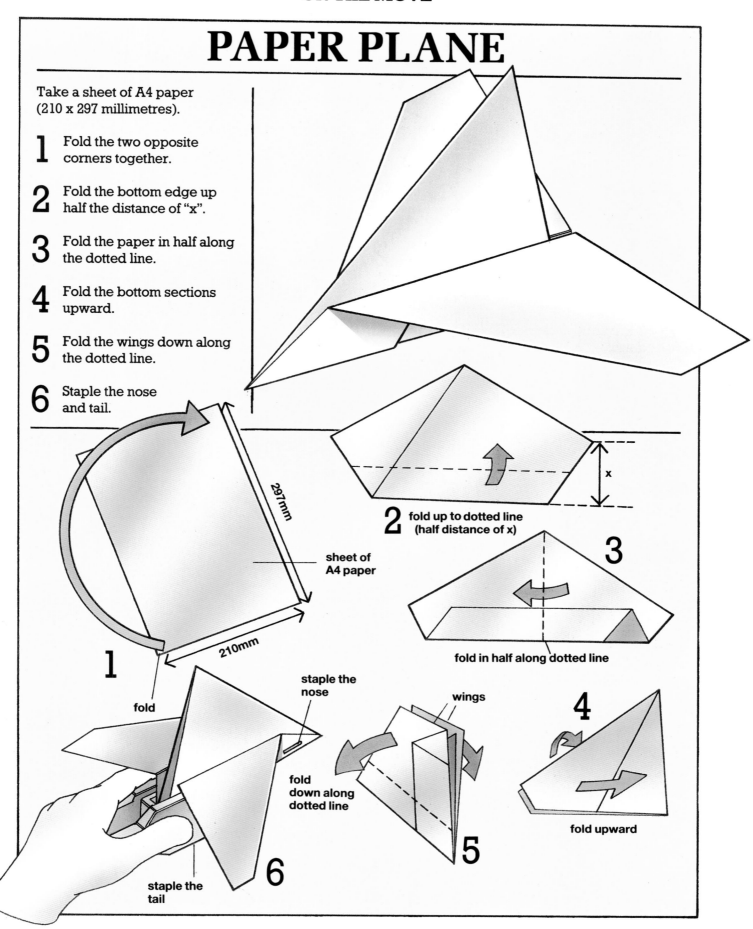

297mm

sheet of A4 paper

210mm

1 fold

2 fold up to dotted line (half distance of x)

x

3 fold in half along dotted line

4 fold upward

5 wings
fold down along dotted line

6 staple the nose
staple the tail

PAPER DART

Use one sheet of A4 paper to make a paper dart.

1 Fold in half.

2 Open out and fold the corner over.

3 Fold the other corner over.

4 Fold the paper again, like this.

5 Turn the other corner down.

6 Turn over.

7 Fold sides to centre.

8 Fold again.

9 Fold in half.

10 Hold the centre fold and open out.

11 Fix the paper dart with sticky tape.

12 Launch it.

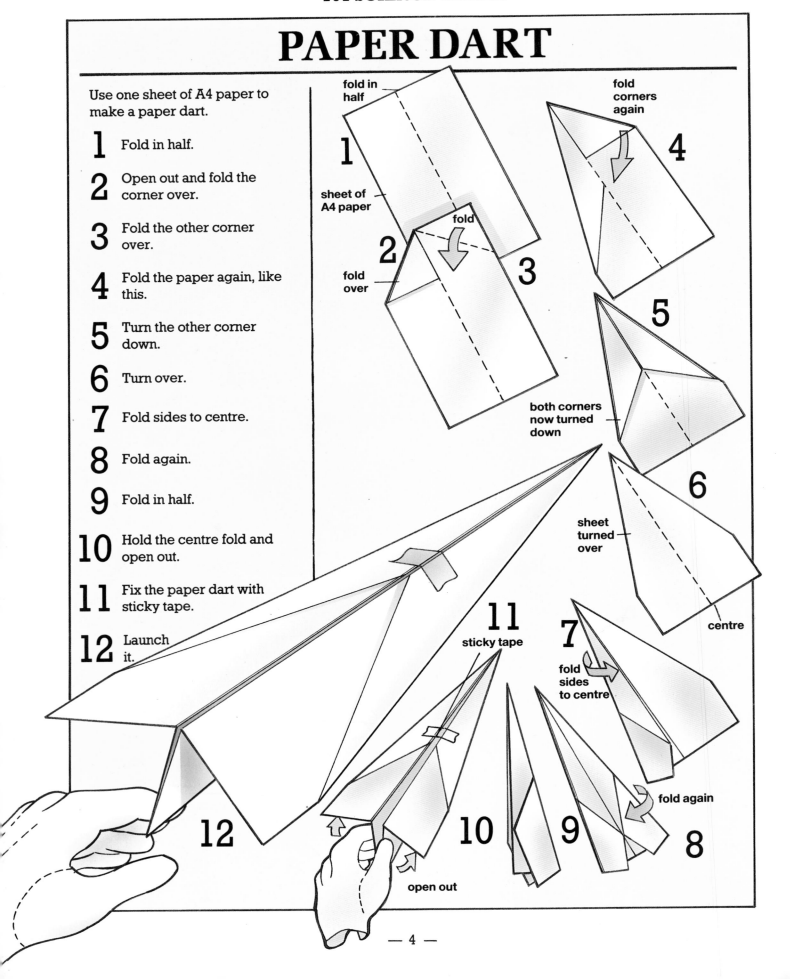

IMPROVING FLIGHT

Very often the dart will not fly well. It needs balancing. Fix a paper-clip to the body of the dart to give a good balance about its centre, as shown right.

1 Add tail flaps to the dart as shown, below right.

2 Fly with the flaps up. Fly with the flaps down.

3 Fold to make stabilizers. Add stabilizers.

4 Try stabilizers both up and down.

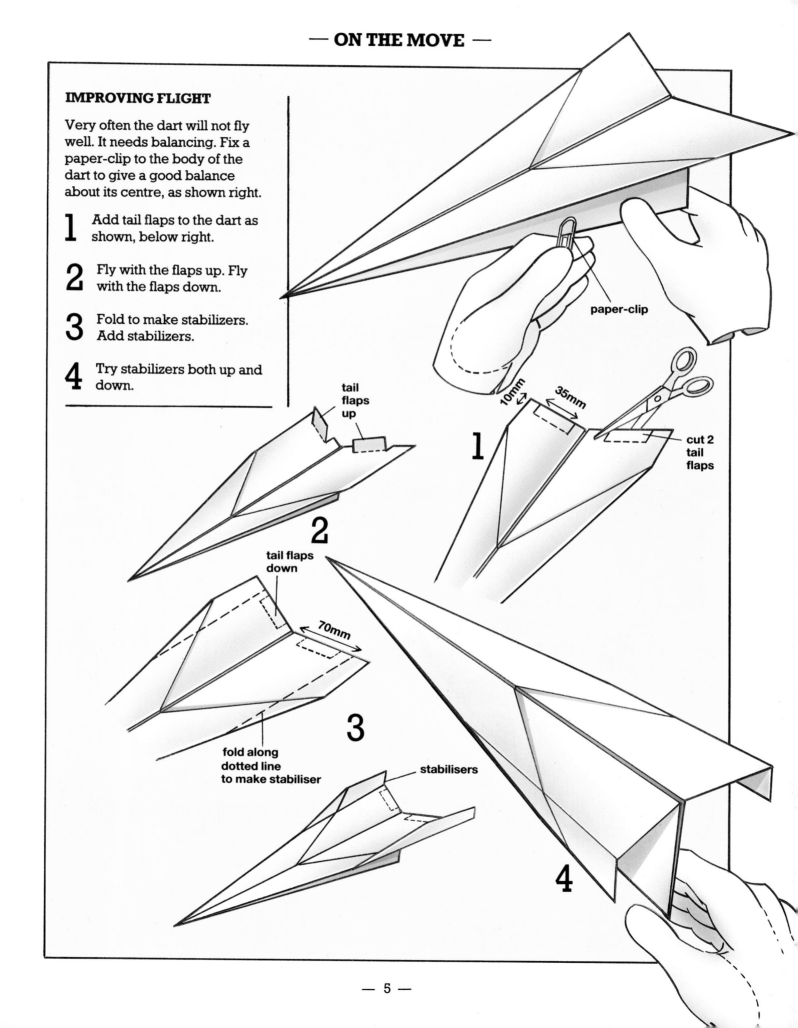

paper-clip

1

10mm   35mm

cut 2 tail flaps

tail flaps up

2

tail flaps down

70mm

3

fold along dotted line to make stabiliser

stabilisers

4

DELTA WING

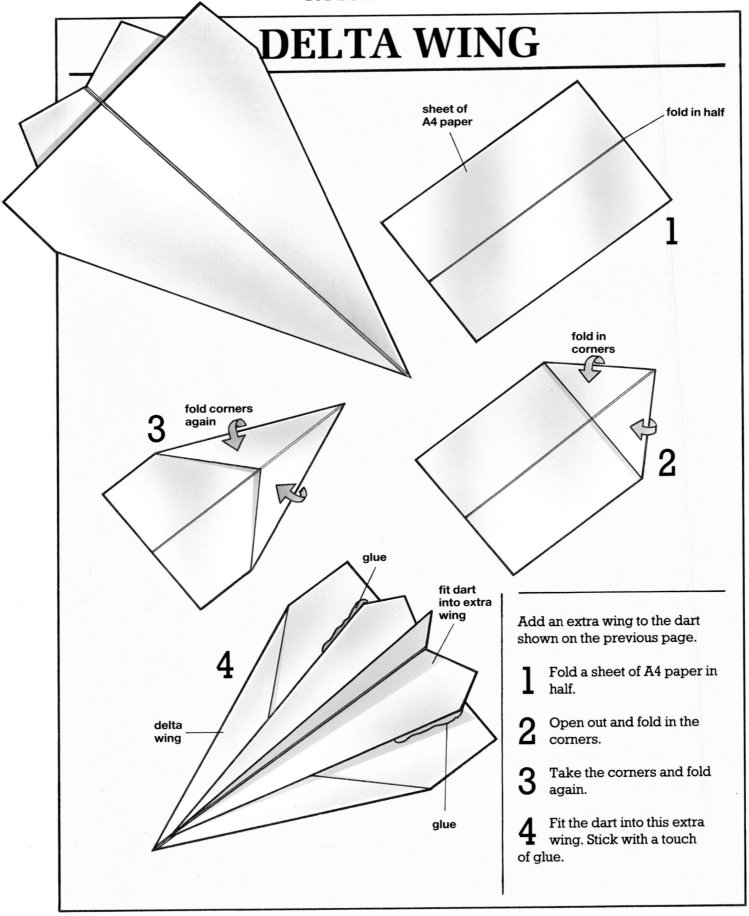

sheet of A4 paper

fold in half

1

fold in corners

2

fold corners again

3

glue

fit dart into extra wing

4

delta wing

glue

Add an extra wing to the dart shown on the previous page.

1 Fold a sheet of A4 paper in half.

2 Open out and fold in the corners.

3 Take the corners and fold again.

4 Fit the dart into this extra wing. Stick with a touch of glue.

ACROBATIC PLANE

1 Fold a sheet of A4 paper crosswise.

2 Open up and fold a crease 13 millimetres from the edge of the long side.

3 Fold and fold again several times.

4 Refold to centre line. Cut out a notch in the paper as below.

5 Open out the acrobatic plane.

6 Fold the wing tips of the plane up.

7 Fold down the outer edges of the tail.

8 Check the plane for symmetry. It is essential that one half is a mirror image of the other.

9 Launch the plane gently away from you with a slight downward motion.

TIPS

1 If the plane glides all right but moves from side to side check the symmetry.

2 If the plane dives turn the trailing edge of the tail up a little.

3 If the plane undulates turn the trailing edges of the tail down. If this is not successful the plane may be too heavy in the tail. Try a tiny piece of Plasticine or a paper-clip on the nose.

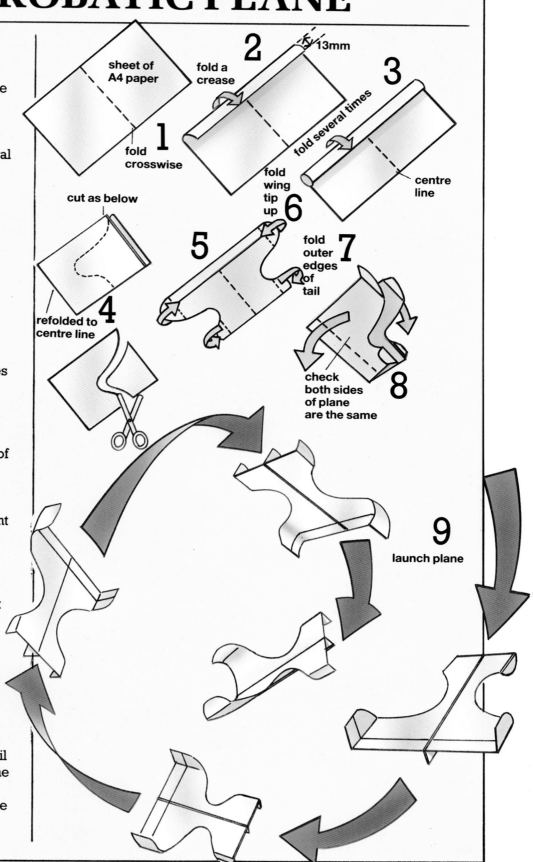

sheet of A4 paper — fold crosswise — **1**

13mm — fold a crease — **2**

fold several times — centre line — **3**

cut as below — refolded to centre line — **4**

5

fold wing tip up — **6**

fold outer edges of tail — **7**

check both sides of plane are the same — **8**

launch plane — **9**

BALSA WOOD GLIDER

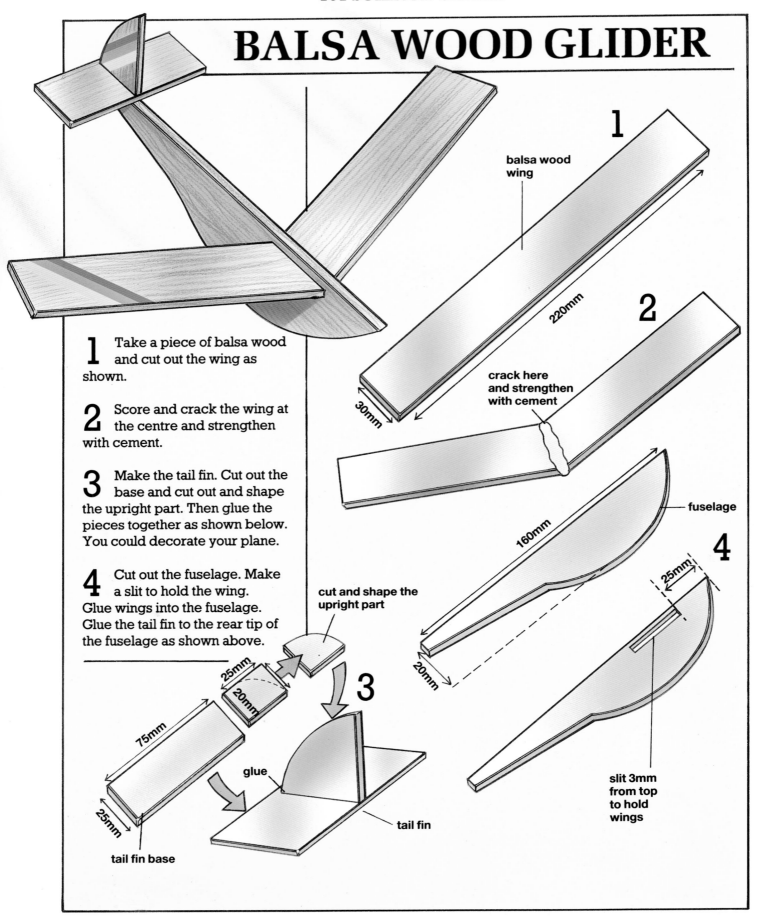

1 Take a piece of balsa wood and cut out the wing as shown.

2 Score and crack the wing at the centre and strengthen with cement.

3 Make the tail fin. Cut out the base and cut out and shape the upright part. Then glue the pieces together as shown below. You could decorate your plane.

4 Cut out the fuselage. Make a slit to hold the wing. Glue wings into the fuselage. Glue the tail fin to the rear tip of the fuselage as shown above.

balsa wood wing

220mm

30mm

crack here and strengthen with cement

fuselage

160mm

20mm

25mm

slit 3mm from top to hold wings

cut and shape the upright part

25mm

20mm

75mm

25mm

tail fin base

glue

tail fin

JET ROCKET

This balloon rocket runs on nylon fishing line fixed tightly across a room.

1 Thread two short pieces of drinking straw onto the line.

2 Blow up the balloon. Close the neck of the balloon with a bulldog clip.

3 Tape the straws to the inflated balloon with sticky tape. Make sure the fishing line is taut and straight.

4 When you are ready to launch your rocket, remove the clip to release the balloon.

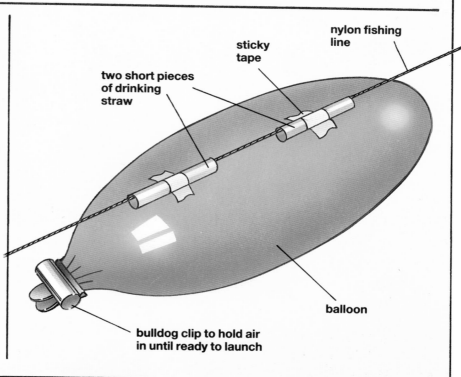

nylon fishing line

sticky tape

two short pieces of drinking straw

balloon

bulldog clip to hold air in until ready to launch

PROPELLER-DRIVEN PLANE

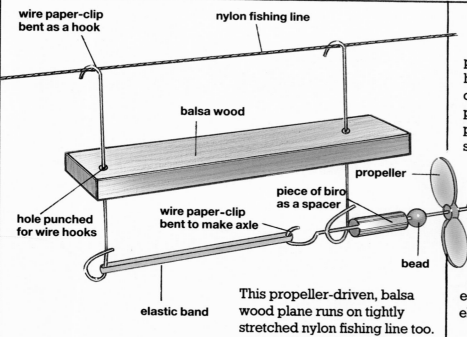

wire paper-clip bent as a hook

nylon fishing line

balsa wood

hole punched for wire hooks

wire paper-clip bent to make axle

piece of biro as a spacer

propeller

bead

elastic band

1 Use a wire paper-clip to make the axle to hold the propeller. You need a bead to help it run smoothly and a piece of Biro as a spacer. Thread the piece of Biro and the bead and propeller onto your wire axle as shown.

2 Bend two other paper-clips to make the wire hooks that pass through the balsa wood body of the plane.

3 Wind the propeller round and round to twist the elastic band and give the plane elastic energy.

4 Release the propeller and watch the plane whizz along.

This propeller-driven, balsa wood plane runs on tightly stretched nylon fishing line too. The propeller needs to be bought from a hobby shop.

PARACHUTES

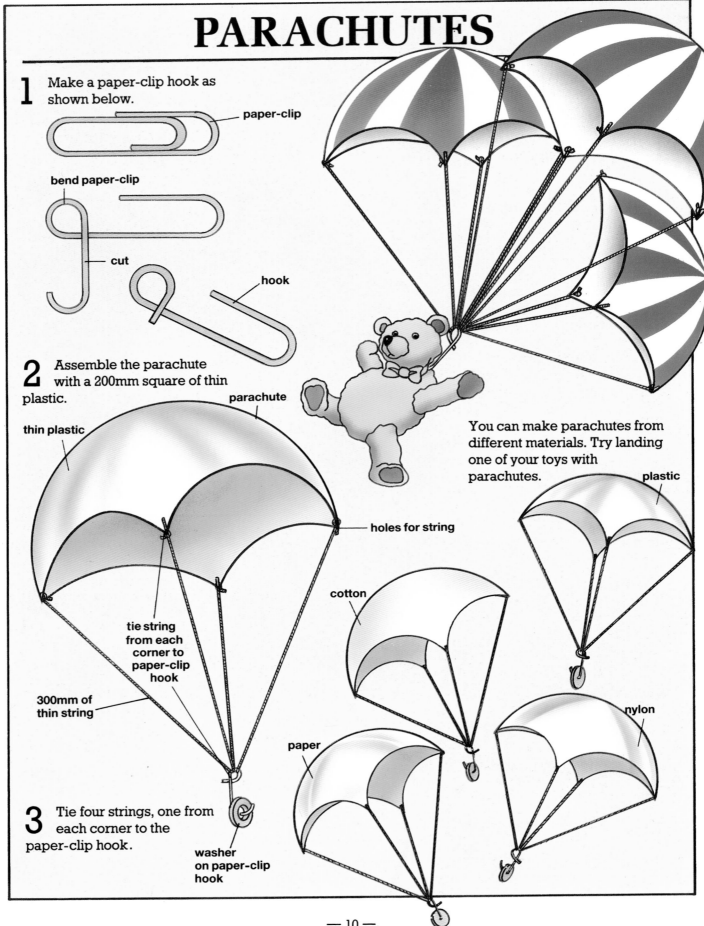

1 Make a paper-clip hook as shown below.

paper-clip

bend paper-clip

cut

hook

2 Assemble the parachute with a 200mm square of thin plastic.

thin plastic

parachute

holes for string

tie string from each corner to paper-clip hook

300mm of thin string

You can make parachutes from different materials. Try landing one of your toys with parachutes.

plastic

cotton

nylon

paper

3 Tie four strings, one from each corner to the paper-clip hook.

washer on paper-clip hook

PAPER SPINNERS

1 Take a sheet of notepaper (120 × 90mm.) Make two 100mm slits by cutting along the dotted lines as shown.

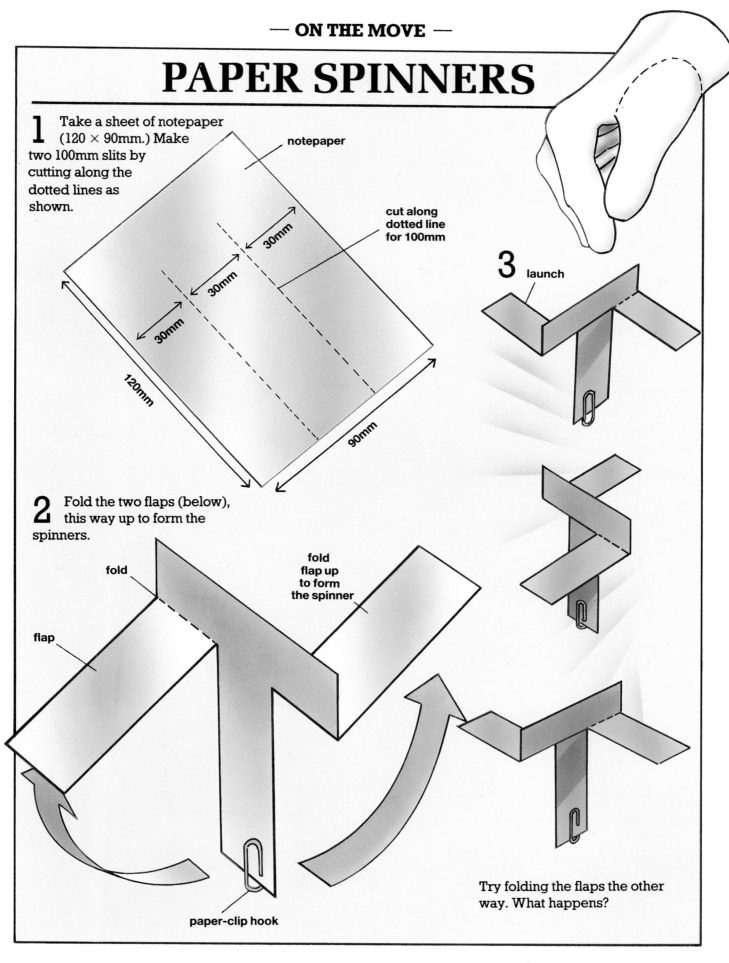

notepaper

cut along dotted line for 100mm

30mm
30mm
30mm

120mm

90mm

3 launch

2 Fold the two flaps (below), this way up to form the spinners.

fold

flap

fold flap up to form the spinner

paper-clip hook

Try folding the flaps the other way. What happens?

BOOMERANGS

1 Trace the outline of this boomerang onto card. Cut it out.

2 Bend the tip AB just a slight bend.

3 Flick the boomerang from the back of a book. You will need to experiment with the angle you hold the book.

Persevere!

If the bend in the tip is slight, the boomerang will fly in a large orbit. If the bend is more pronounced, the boomerang will have a smaller flying circle.

4 The Y shape does not look like a boomerang. However, it is just as effective. Trace the outline onto card. Cut it out.

5 Flick the Y shape from the back of a book. Again you will need to experiment with the angle of launch. Practice makes perfect!

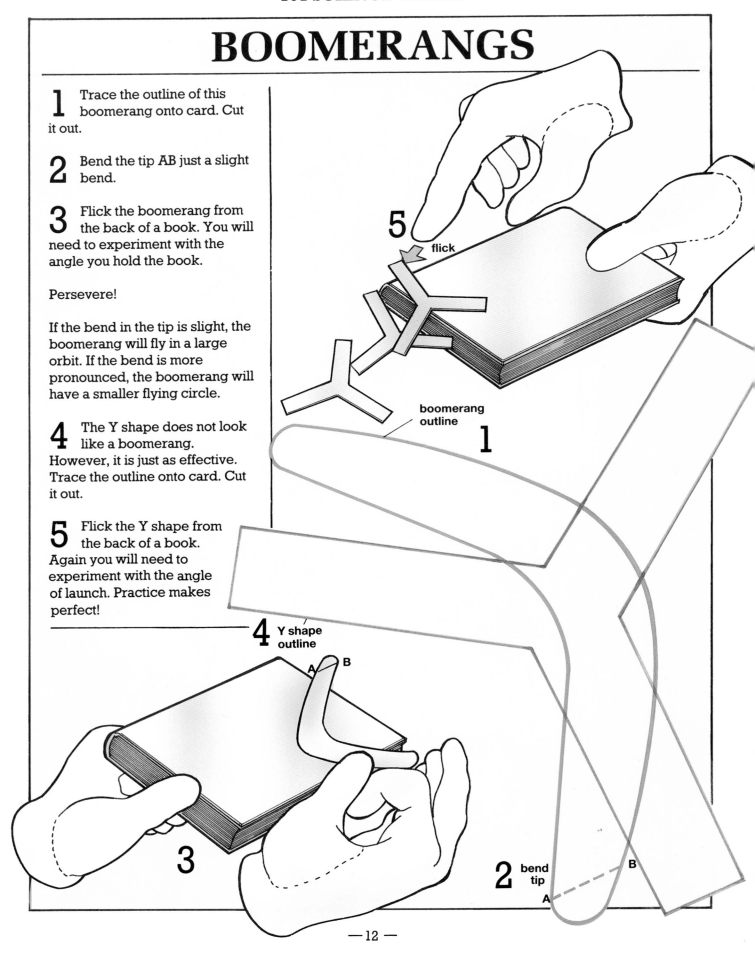

5 flick

boomerang outline

1

4 Y shape outline

A B

3

2 bend tip

A B

WINDMILLS

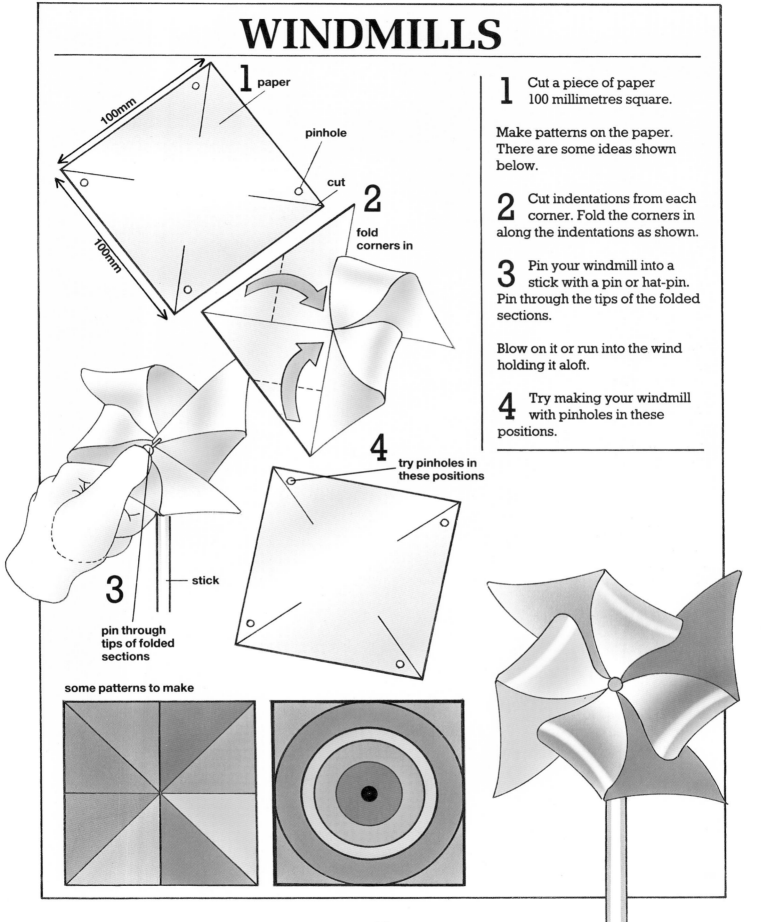

1 paper

100mm

100mm

pinhole

cut

2 fold corners in

3 pin through tips of folded sections

stick

4 try pinholes in these positions

some patterns to make

1 Cut a piece of paper 100 millimetres square.

Make patterns on the paper. There are some ideas shown below.

2 Cut indentations from each corner. Fold the corners in along the indentations as shown.

3 Pin your windmill into a stick with a pin or hat-pin. Pin through the tips of the folded sections.

Blow on it or run into the wind holding it aloft.

4 Try making your windmill with pinholes in these positions.

TIN HELICOPTER

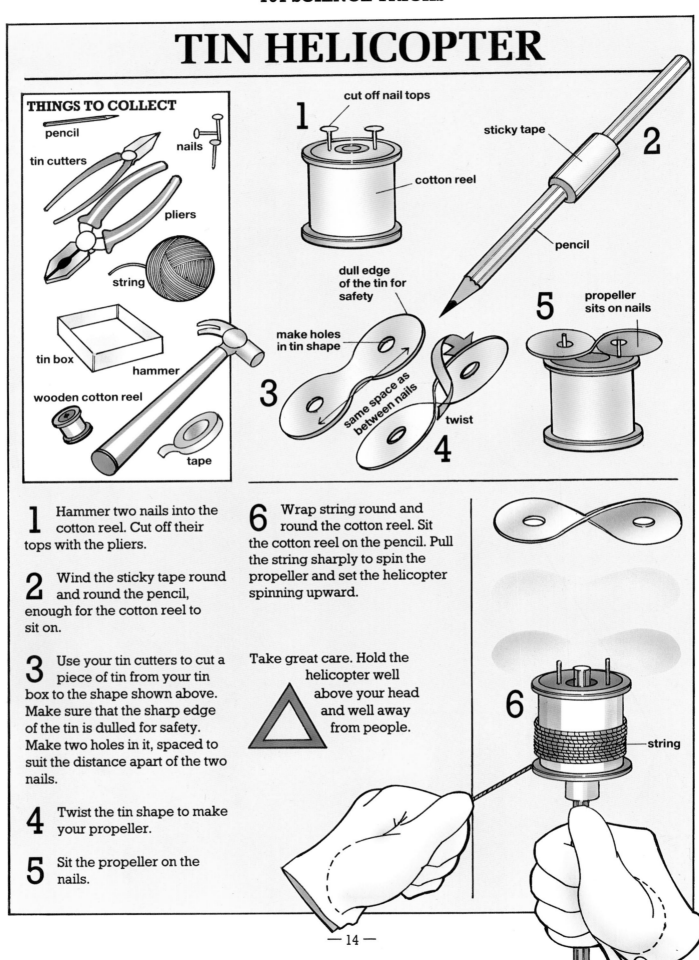

THINGS TO COLLECT

pencil

nails

tin cutters

pliers

string

tin box

hammer

wooden cotton reel

tape

1 cut off nail tops

cotton reel

2 sticky tape

pencil

3 dull edge of the tin for safety

make holes in tin shape

same space as between nails

4 twist

5 propeller sits on nails

1 Hammer two nails into the cotton reel. Cut off their tops with the pliers.

2 Wind the sticky tape round and round the pencil, enough for the cotton reel to sit on.

3 Use your tin cutters to cut a piece of tin from your tin box to the shape shown above. Make sure that the sharp edge of the tin is dulled for safety. Make two holes in it, spaced to suit the distance apart of the two nails.

4 Twist the tin shape to make your propeller.

5 Sit the propeller on the nails.

6 Wrap string round and round the cotton reel. Sit the cotton reel on the pencil. Pull the string sharply to spin the propeller and set the helicopter spinning upward.

Take great care. Hold the helicopter well above your head and well away from people.

6 string

PLASTIC HELICOPTER

Take any flat-sided plastic container.

1 Use a pair of scissors to cut a strip of plastic from this flat-sided container.

2 Make a hole through the centre of the plastic strip with a nail.

3 Push a pencil through the plastic. Twist the plastic strip slightly to make your helicopter.

4 Spin the helicopter in your hand and throw it into the air.

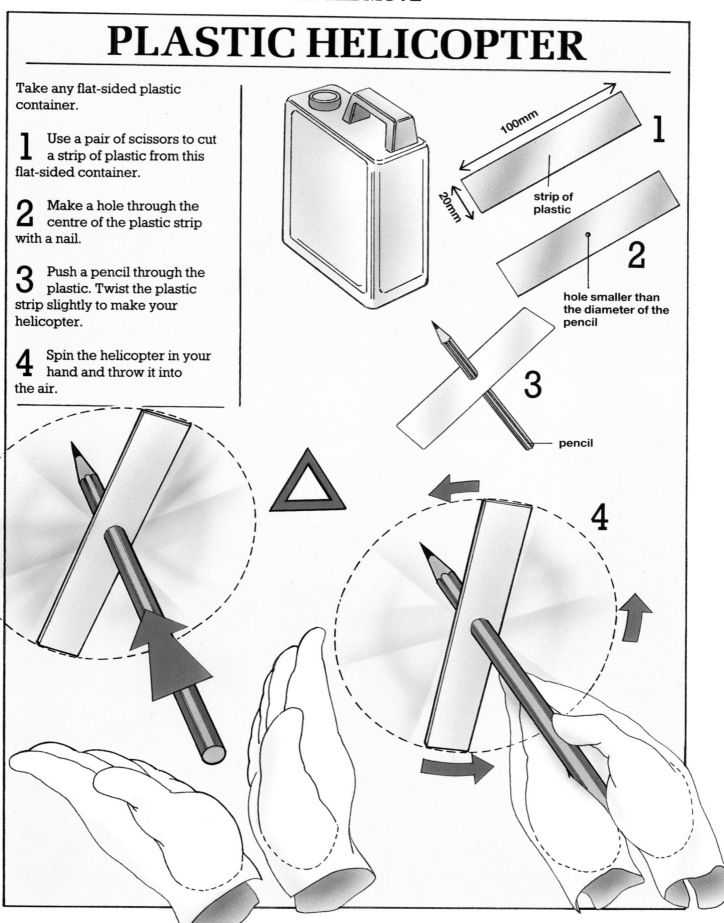

100mm

20mm

1

strip of plastic

2

hole smaller than the diameter of the pencil

3

pencil

4

KITE

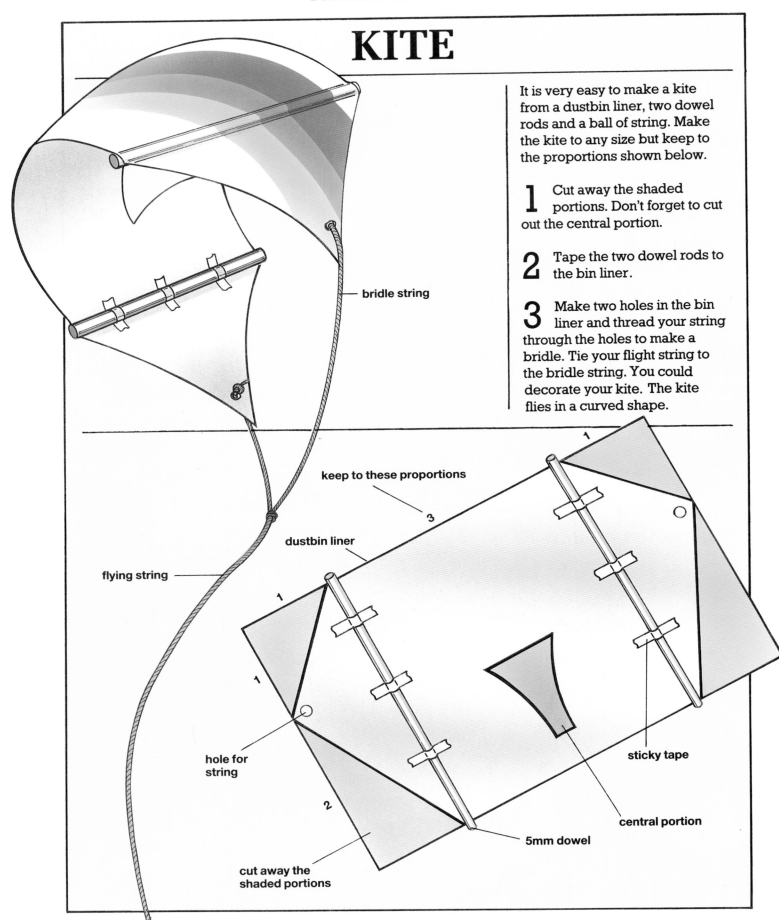

It is very easy to make a kite from a dustbin liner, two dowel rods and a ball of string. Make the kite to any size but keep to the proportions shown below.

1 Cut away the shaded portions. Don't forget to cut out the central portion.

2 Tape the two dowel rods to the bin liner.

3 Make two holes in the bin liner and thread your string through the holes to make a bridle. Tie your flight string to the bridle string. You could decorate your kite. The kite flies in a curved shape.

bridle string

keep to these proportions

dustbin liner

flying string

hole for string

cut away the shaded portions

5mm dowel

sticky tape

central portion

HOT-AIR BALLOON

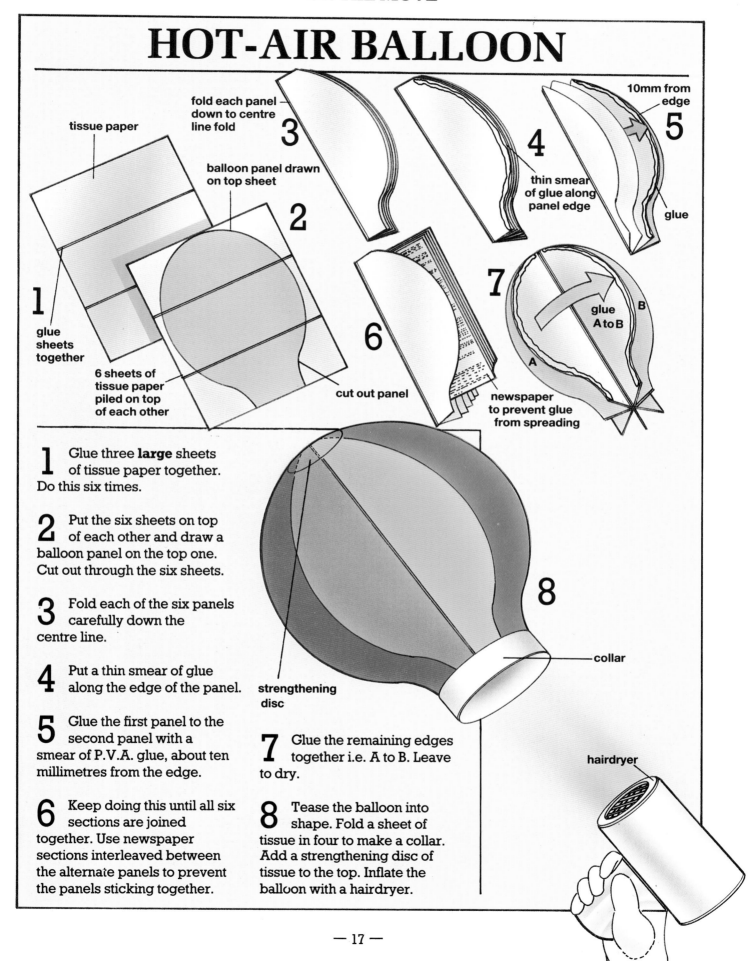

tissue paper

fold each panel down to centre line fold

3

4

10mm from edge

5

balloon panel drawn on top sheet

2

thin smear of glue along panel edge

glue

1

glue sheets together

6 sheets of tissue paper piled on top of each other

6

7

glue A to B

B

A

cut out panel

newspaper to prevent glue from spreading

strengthening disc

8

collar

hairdryer

1 Glue three **large** sheets of tissue paper together. Do this six times.

2 Put the six sheets on top of each other and draw a balloon panel on the top one. Cut out through the six sheets.

3 Fold each of the six panels carefully down the centre line.

4 Put a thin smear of glue along the edge of the panel.

5 Glue the first panel to the second panel with a smear of P.V.A. glue, about ten millimetres from the edge.

6 Keep doing this until all six sections are joined together. Use newspaper sections interleaved between the alternate panels to prevent the panels sticking together.

7 Glue the remaining edges together i.e. A to B. Leave to dry.

8 Tease the balloon into shape. Fold a sheet of tissue in four to make a collar. Add a strengthening disc of tissue to the top. Inflate the balloon with a hairdryer.

COTTON-REEL TANK

THINGS TO COLLECT

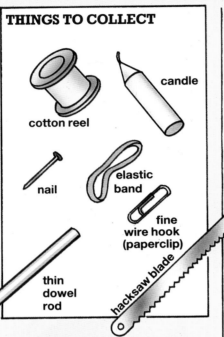

candle

cotton reel

nail

elastic band

fine wire hook (paperclip)

thin dowel rod

hacksaw blade

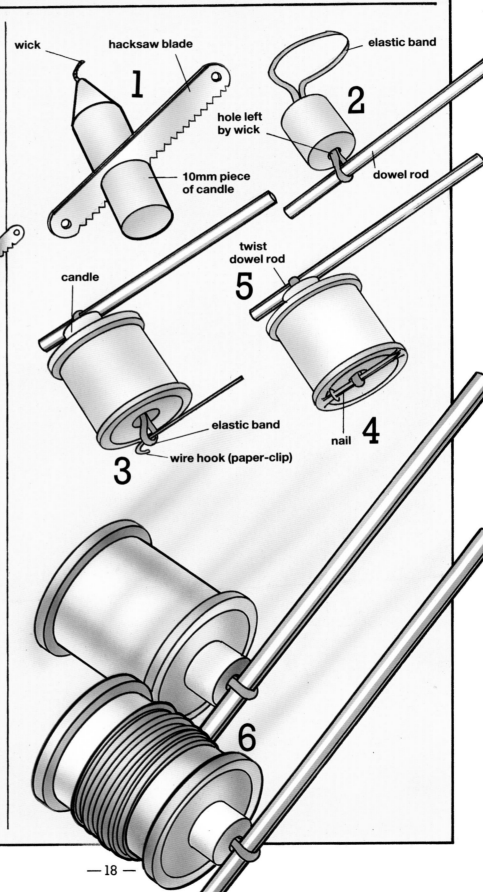

1 wick, hacksaw blade, 10mm piece of candle

2 elastic band, hole left by wick, dowel rod

3 candle, elastic band, wire hook (paper-clip)

5 twist dowel rod

4 nail

6

1 Cut a 10 millimetre piece off the candle. Check with a parent or teacher first before you use the hacksaw. They may need to cut the candle for you. Use the hacksaw blade with a gentle sawing action.

2 Make a hole through the centre of the candle by pulling out the wick. Thread the elastic band through the candle and secure it with the dowel.

3 Pull the free end of the elastic band through the cotton reel with the wire hook.

4 Secure the free end of the elastic band with a nail.

5 Wind the elastic by twisting the dowel rod round and round. Place the cotton reel tank on the ground and watch it move.

6 Wind with elastic band to help the tank grip when climbing slopes.

DRINK CAN DRAGSTER

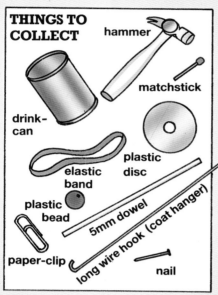

THINGS TO COLLECT

hammer

matchstick

drink-can

elastic band

plastic disc

plastic bead

5mm dowel

paper-clip

long wire hook (coat hanger)

nail

1 Make a hole through the blank end of the can with a nail.

2 Straighten out the paper-clip to make a hook.

3 Put the hook through the disc and the plastic bead.

4 Bend the straight end of the wire on the dowel rod and twist it around.

5 Use the long wire hook to pull an elastic band through the can.

6 Secure the other end of the elastic band to a matchstick.

7 Wind the rod round and round so that the elastic winds tightly and then release the dragster.

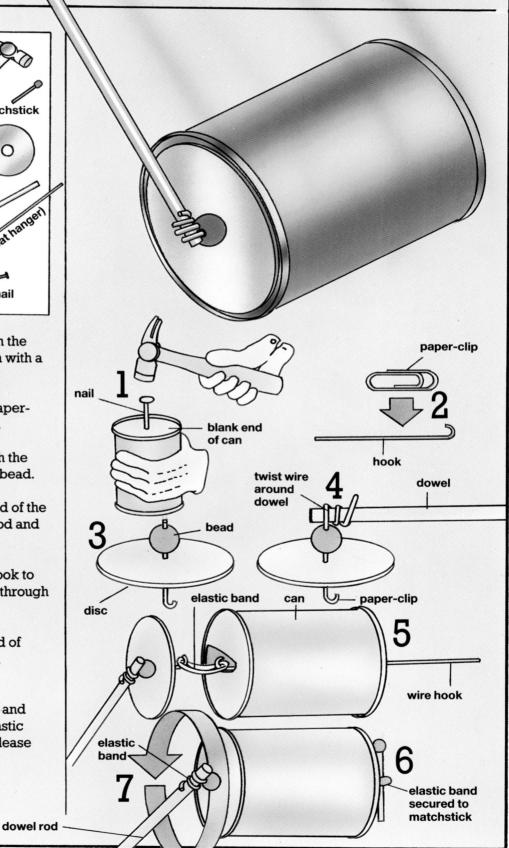

paper-clip

1

nail

blank end of can

2

hook

dowel

twist wire around dowel

4

3

bead

disc

elastic band

can

paper-clip

5

wire hook

elastic band

7

6

elastic band secured to matchstick

dowel rod

LAND YACHT

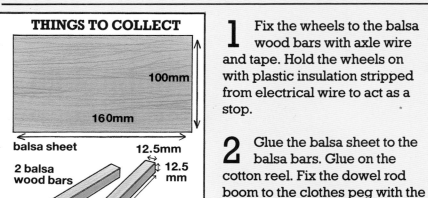

100mm

160mm

balsa sheet

12.5mm

12.5 mm

2 balsa wood bars

100mm

4 model plane wheels

reel

peg

two thin dowel rods

plastic covered wire

tape

dustbin liner

1 Fix the wheels to the balsa wood bars with axle wire and tape. Hold the wheels on with plastic insulation stripped from electrical wire to act as a stop.

2 Glue the balsa sheet to the balsa bars. Glue on the cotton reel. Fix the dowel rod boom to the clothes peg with the elastic bands. Put the dowel rod mast into the centre of the cotton reel. Fix the boom to the mast with the clothes peg.

3 Cut and fix a piece of bin liner as a sail. You could use other material if you wish. Decorate your sail. Try your land yacht on a hard flat surface when there is some wind.

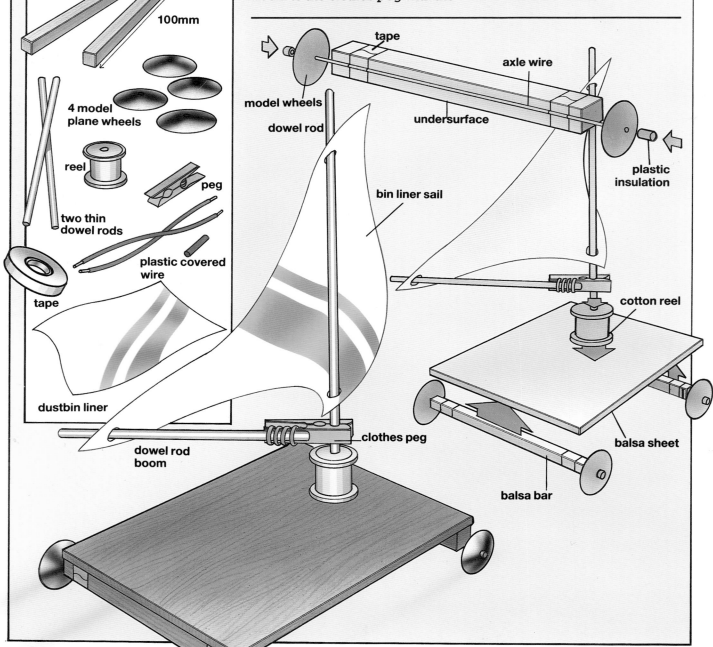

tape

axle wire

model wheels

undersurface

dowel rod

plastic insulation

bin liner sail

cotton reel

clothes peg

dowel rod boom

balsa sheet

balsa bar

TROLLEY

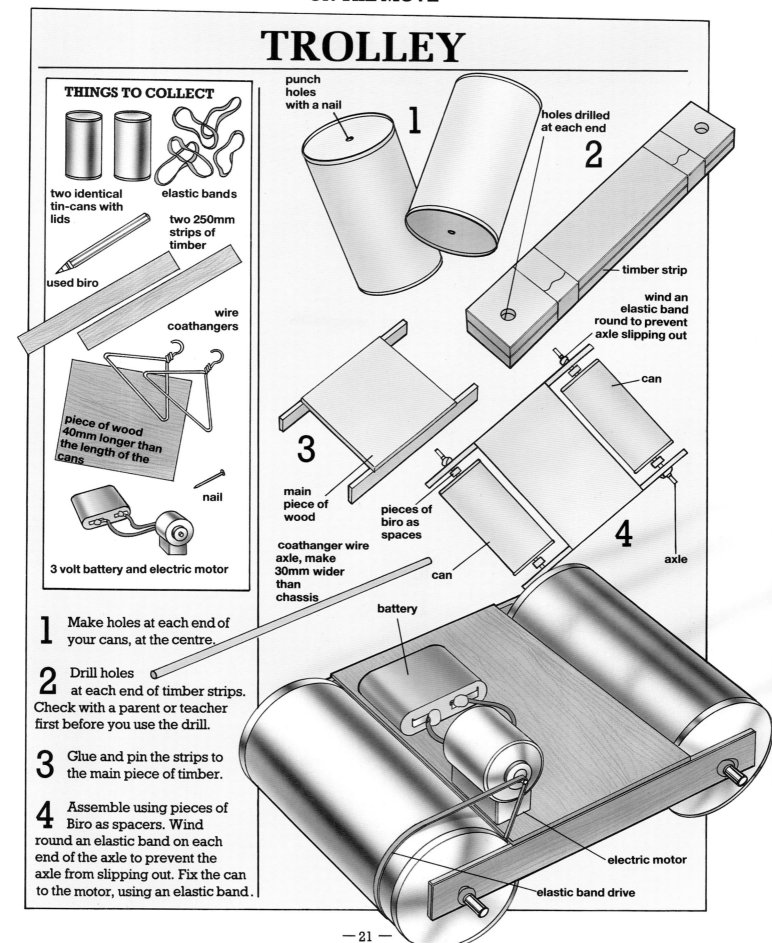

THINGS TO COLLECT

two identical tin-cans with lids

elastic bands

used biro

two 250mm strips of timber

wire coathangers

piece of wood 40mm longer than the length of the cans

nail

3 volt battery and electric motor

punch holes with a nail

1

holes drilled at each end

2

timber strip

wind an elastic band round to prevent axle slipping out

can

3

main piece of wood

pieces of biro as spaces

can

4

axle

coathanger wire axle, make 30mm wider than chassis

battery

electric motor

elastic band drive

1 Make holes at each end of your cans, at the centre.

2 Drill holes at each end of timber strips. Check with a parent or teacher first before you use the drill.

3 Glue and pin the strips to the main piece of timber.

4 Assemble using pieces of Biro as spacers. Wind round an elastic band on each end of the axle to prevent the axle from slipping out. Fix the can to the motor, using an elastic band.

JUMPING JACK

1 Trace these pieces of the Jack's body, (below), onto card. Cut them out and decorate them.

2 Fix the arms and legs to the main body with paper fasteners. Make small holes in the arms, legs and main body with the point of a Biro, and attach the string as shown.

3 Make a small hole in the Jack's head and attach the string to the head as shown. Hold the Jack by the string from the head. Pull the lower string to make him jump.

2 paper fasteners

small holes for string

3

string

1

arms

outline of main body

legs

cut shapes from card

MOUSE ON THE MOVE

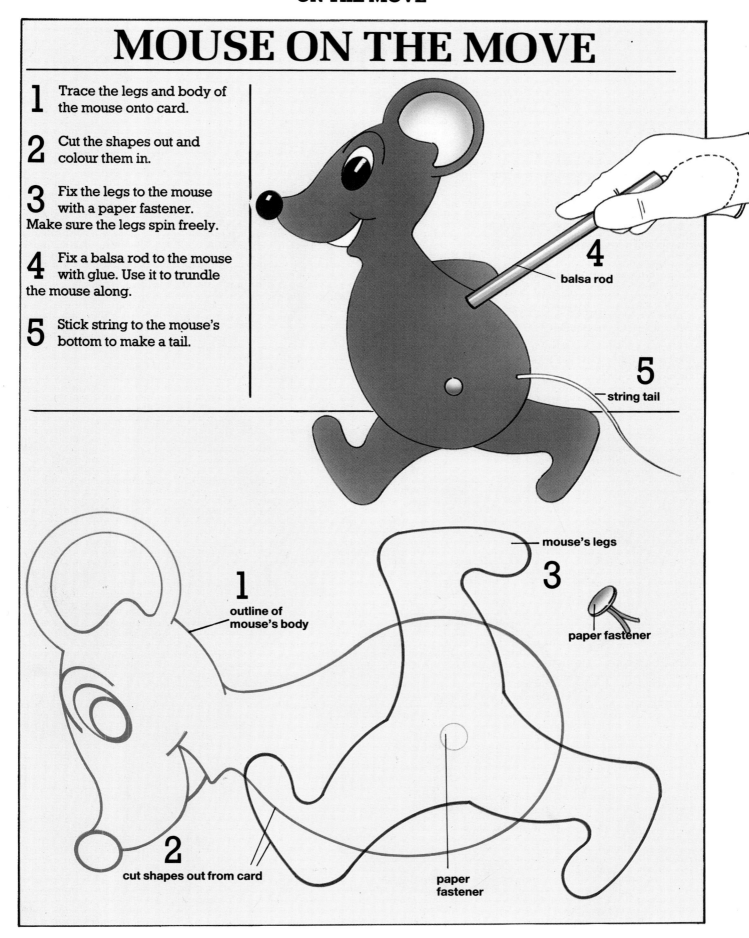

1 Trace the legs and body of the mouse onto card.

2 Cut the shapes out and colour them in.

3 Fix the legs to the mouse with a paper fastener. Make sure the legs spin freely.

4 Fix a balsa rod to the mouse with glue. Use it to trundle the mouse along.

5 Stick string to the mouse's bottom to make a tail.

4 balsa rod

5 string tail

1 outline of mouse's body

2 cut shapes out from card

3 mouse's legs

paper fastener

paper fastener

TOPS

Make some tops from card.

1 Take a pair of compasses and draw some circles about 80 millimetres in diameter.

2 Decorate these circles. Make up different designs and coloured patterns as shown.

3 Cut your coloured circles out. Push a piece of dowel rod or a pencil through the centre of each circle to act as a spindle.

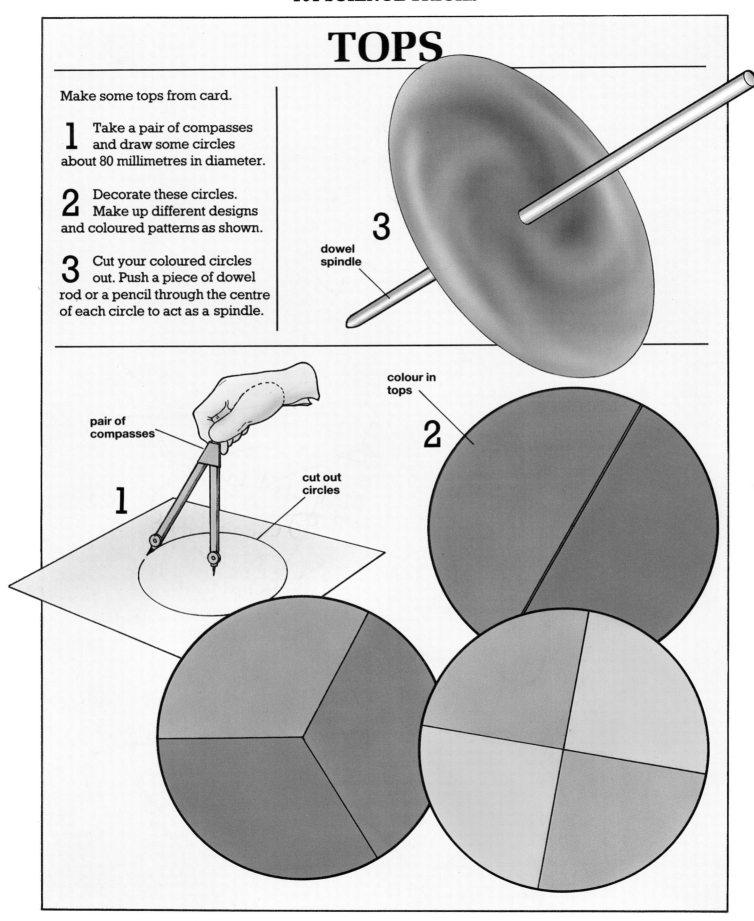

3

dowel spindle

colour in tops

2

pair of compasses

1

cut out circles

DESIGNS AND PATTERNS

Try spinning your tops.
See what happens to
the colours and
patterns as they
spin.

SPINNERS

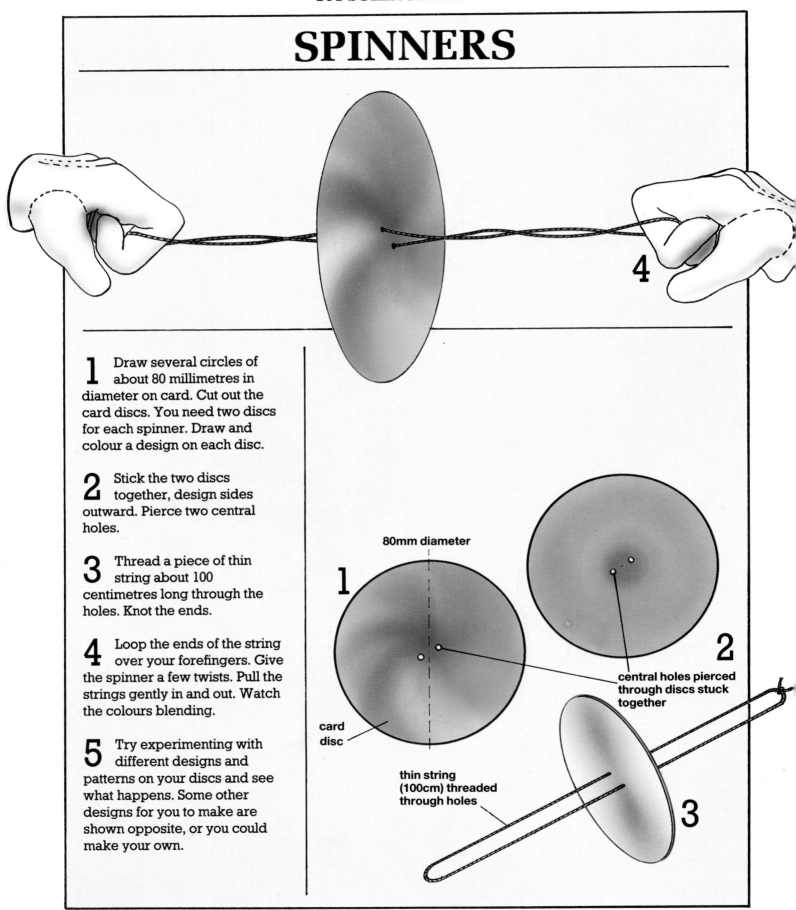

1 Draw several circles of about 80 millimetres in diameter on card. Cut out the card discs. You need two discs for each spinner. Draw and colour a design on each disc.

2 Stick the two discs together, design sides outward. Pierce two central holes.

3 Thread a piece of thin string about 100 centimetres long through the holes. Knot the ends.

4 Loop the ends of the string over your forefingers. Give the spinner a few twists. Pull the strings gently in and out. Watch the colours blending.

5 Try experimenting with different designs and patterns on your discs and see what happens. Some other designs for you to make are shown opposite, or you could make your own.

80mm diameter

card disc

central holes pierced through discs stuck together

thin string (100cm) threaded through holes

MAKE OTHER DESIGNS

5

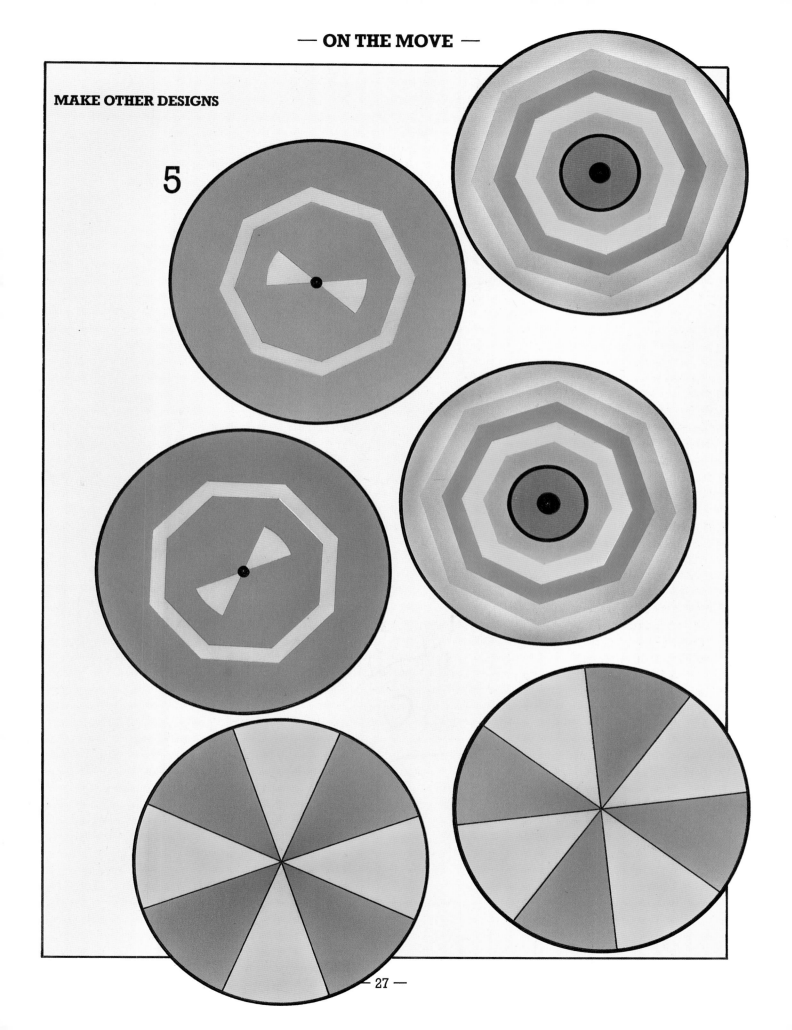

PAPER BOAT

1 Use a sheet of greaseproof paper 200 millimetres square. Fold the sides to the middle.

2 Fold in the corners to the middle.

3 Make creases, as shown, and fold in.

4 Crease horizontally across, as shown, and fold in.

5 Turn the boat over – inside out so to speak!

Float the boat along a stream or in the bath.

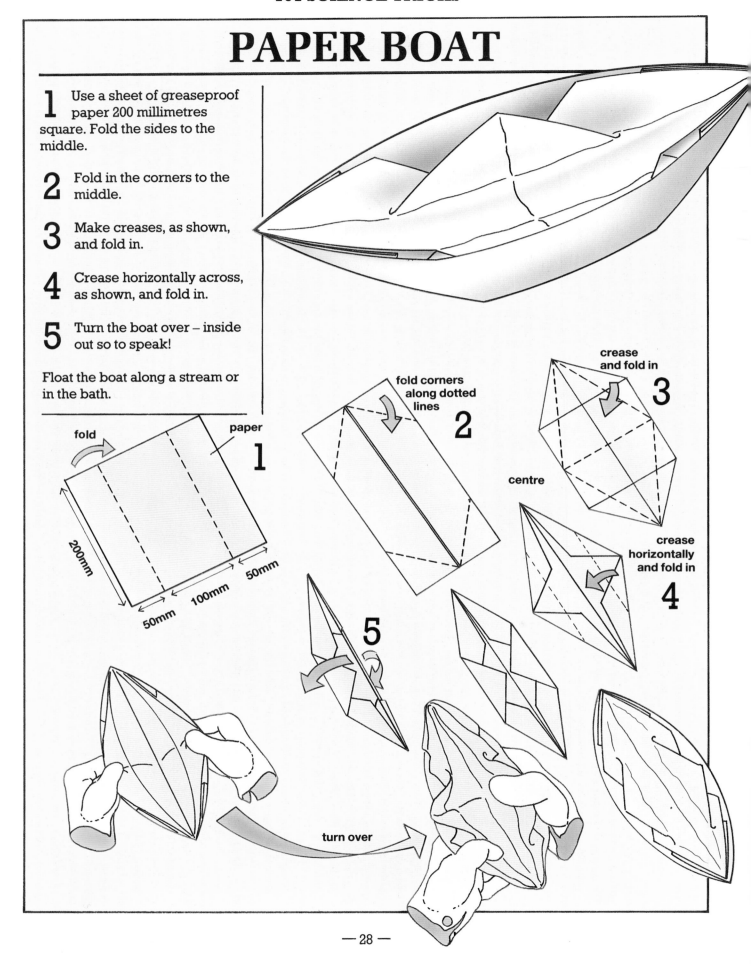

BALSA WOOD BOATS

1 You need some balsa wood to make the bases or 'hulls' of your boats. Look at the different shaped hulls below and choose some shapes to try. Cut them out.

2 Make sails for your boats with knitting needles and paper. Look at the different shaped sails below and choose some shapes to try. Cut out the sails from paper and attach them to your hulls with knitting needles.

Small sails for small boats can be made from cocktail sticks and paper.

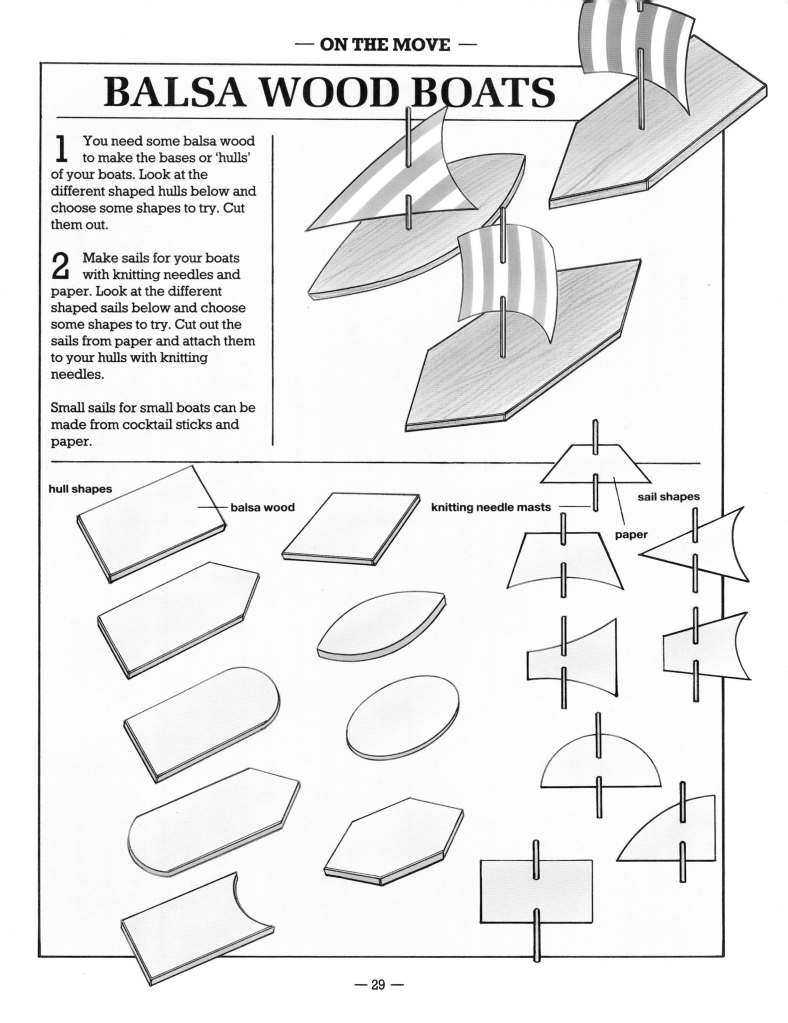

hull shapes

balsa wood

knitting needle masts

sail shapes

paper

POWER-DRIVEN BOATS

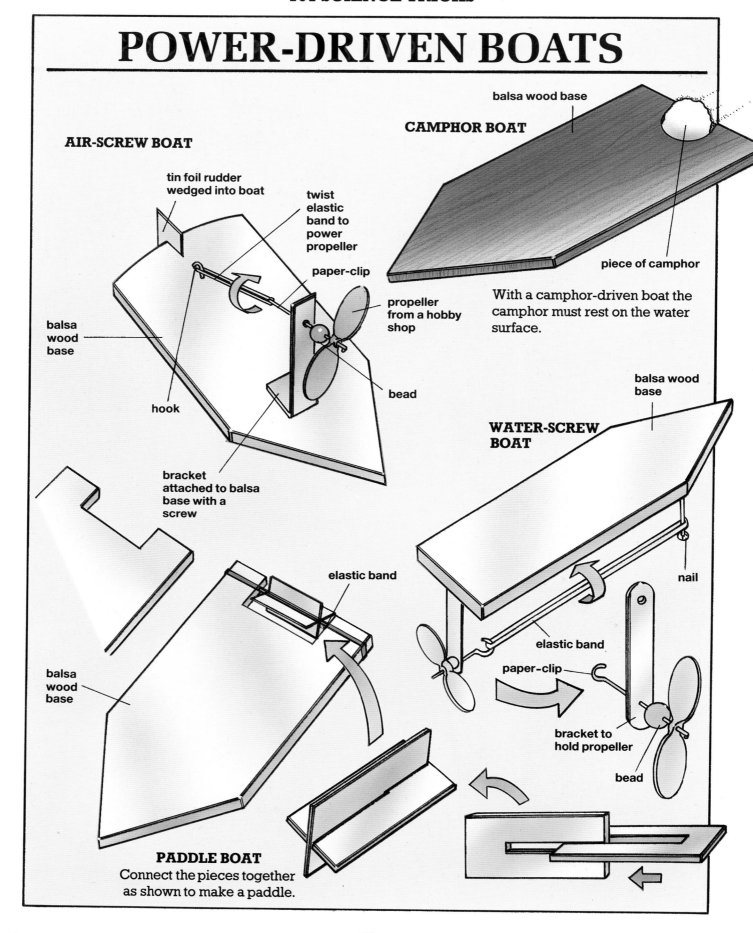

CAMPHOR BOAT

balsa wood base

piece of camphor

With a camphor-driven boat the camphor must rest on the water surface.

AIR-SCREW BOAT

tin foil rudder wedged into boat

twist elastic band to power propeller

paper-clip

propeller from a hobby shop

balsa wood base

hook

bead

bracket attached to balsa base with a screw

WATER-SCREW BOAT

balsa wood base

nail

elastic band

paper-clip

bracket to hold propeller

bead

balsa wood base

elastic band

PADDLE BOAT
Connect the pieces together as shown to make a paddle.

CATAMARAN AND TRIMARAN

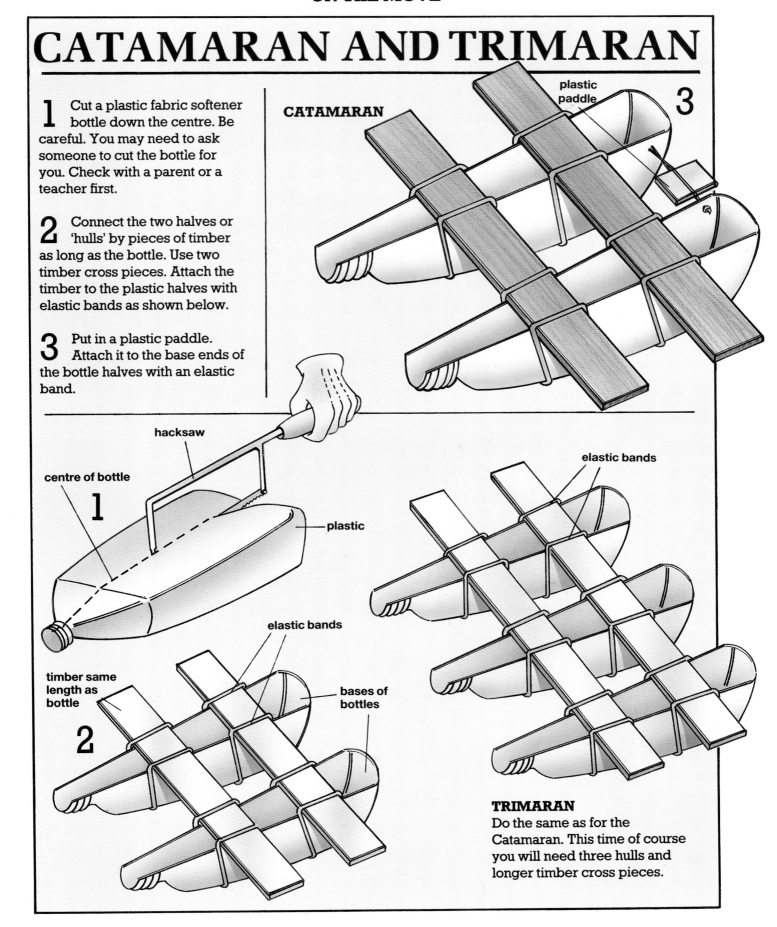

1 Cut a plastic fabric softener bottle down the centre. Be careful. You may need to ask someone to cut the bottle for you. Check with a parent or a teacher first.

2 Connect the two halves or 'hulls' by pieces of timber as long as the bottle. Use two timber cross pieces. Attach the timber to the plastic halves with elastic bands as shown below.

3 Put in a plastic paddle. Attach it to the base ends of the bottle halves with an elastic band.

CATAMARAN

plastic paddle

3

hacksaw

centre of bottle

1

plastic

timber same length as bottle

elastic bands

2

bases of bottles

elastic bands

TRIMARAN
Do the same as for the Catamaran. This time of course you will need three hulls and longer timber cross pieces.

NOTES FOR PARENTS AND TEACHERS

Pages 3 – 17   These are concerned with things in the air. If you want to consider the forces that keep paper planes in the air you will need to talk with children about thrust, drag, lift and gravity. Thrust is provided by the aeroplane engine. In a paper plane, of course, it is provided by throwing. Drag is the resistance of the air to flight. It acts along the direction of motion of the aeroplane and opposes it. Lift is another force, it acts more or less perpendicularly to the direction of motion. The shape of an aeroplane wing helps develop lift. Gravity is the pull of the earth acting on the plane.

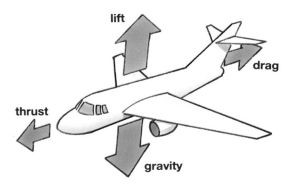

Page 9   Both the models on this page use a form of energy to make them move. The air escaping from the balloon causes it to move forward. To every action there is an equal and opposite reaction. When the balloon is blown up but shut the air inside it presses equally in all directions. When the neck is released the air rushes out and there is no longer any backward pressure. The forward pressure of air on the balloon remains the same however and it travels forward.

forward pressure

The propeller-driven plane moves on 'elastic energy'. Children will have to put the 'energy' in first by winding it up.

Pages 10 – 11   Air pressure is the operative force in making these two models work.

Page 12   The aerodynamics of boomerangs are extremely complex, which is not to say that children cannot get a 'feel' for what is happening by playing with these models.

Page 13   Again we have a toy which works on air pressure.

Pages 14 – 15   The spinning blades from these helicopters cut the air and their curved shape gives them lift, much as an aeroplane wing does.

Do please supervise these activities.

Page 16   The kite, like the aeroplane, is subjected to forces. The energy to lift it provided by the wind, whilst its angle to the wind gives it lift. Like aeroplanes it is subjected to the pull of gravity.

Page 17   Hot-air balloons work on the principle that warm air is less dense than cold air (the molecules are further apart). Being filled with warm air the balloons therefore tend to lift displacing the colder, denser air above them.

Pages 18 – 19   Two toys which are very much concerned with 'elastic energy'. If children are interested you can experiment with the number of turns of the elastic in relation to the distance travelled by each vehicle.

Page 20   Angle of attack of the wind is all important in getting a high speed from the land yacht – and it can travel! So encourage children to get the best angle with their boom.

Page 21   Introduces children to the idea of using an electric motor to make things move.

Pages 22 – 23   Both the jumping Jack and the mouse are based on the principle of the lever. That is to say they are both dependent on the effect of a bar moving about a point.

Pages 24 – 27   You have to put energy into tops to make them spin. Colours in the surface of the top will blend. Theoretically if you have a rainbow coloured top all the colours should merge to give white. In practice, this is impossible since one cannot get pure enough pigments. At best you will get a grey blur. The same applies to the spinners.

Pages 28 – 31   Lots of variables here for children to play with in order to get the best boat. Shapes of hull and sail, and power source whether it be blowing or propeller driven by elastic all come into effect.

Camphor reduces the surface tension of the water and the 'water skin' in front of the boat pulls it forward.